AISLE C

CW00435615

MARC

Published by
M and M Associates

© Copyright 2010

> "As dawn brought forth another day
> The pain had still not gone away.
> When will that happy day begin,
> When pain no longer enters in?"

ISBN No: 978-0-9522787-4-0

DEDICATION:

I would like to dedicate this book and the poems I have written to the Members of All Saints Church Walcott.

ACKNOWLEDGEMENTS:

I would like to sincerely thank the following Walcott Businesses for contributing to the printing costs of this book:-

- Steve Bullimore — The Lighthouse Inn
- Bob and Trish — Walcott Caravan & Chalet Park
- Julian and Trish — The Kingfisher Fish Bar

And a sincere thank you to:-

- Colour Print, Norwich for printing this book

- Maurice, my husband, for all his support and encouragement in the publishing of this book and for taking all the pictures.

Margaret Luckett July 2010   Pictures by Maurice Gray

<u>WALCOTT CHURCH</u>

With its tower of stepped battlements
Walcott Church stands proud and tall
Its unusual V-shaped stair turret
And beautiful font, of Purbeck marble.
A 1920's Art Nouveau Lectern
Inside its rebuilt 15th Century doors.
Complete with an Art Deco Organ
And a Memorial to the First World War,
Adorned with names of local Servicemen
Who gave their lives to save us all.
Originally built in mid-thirteenth Century
With its adorned medieval Screen, so tall,
The old Piscina and Sedilia in the Chancel
Adding to the character within its walls.
This beautiful All Saints Walcott Church
Is always full of light, and welcoming charm
Where surroundings of coast and farmland
Go happily arm in arm.

A SAD LOSS

Bright red flowers stood proud
At the front of the church she knew
Virgin white cloth held the vase
Where the flowers now tenderly stood.

I knew that today would be sad
I knew no more would she be.
She had gone from my life on a cloud
Her life was finished-she had gone from me.

I tenderly watched the flowers
As they laid there beside her now,
One moment of time she was here,
In another – so short – she had gone.

AUTUMN IN AUGUST

The seasons are changing
With trepidation, yet ease
Leaves gently falling
In the light summer breeze.
Is Autumn early?
No – it must be the strength
Of the ever increasing changes
In the winds, from the south.
The Continents are merging
The land shrinking too
The seas are encroaching
But tides continue to flow.
Soon we will all be one island
In this ever-changing world
Where the seasons won't change
But will gently and slowly merge.

WHEN I AM OLD

When I am old
I will remember you.
When I am old
I will still love you.
When I am old
I will still need you.
When I am old
I will still hold you.
When I am old
I hope you'll be old too.
To remember the beautiful life,
That I have just shared with you.

<u>HOMELESS</u>

When we were babies we needed help
When we were children, we resented help
When we were parents, we gave help
When we are old, we won't accept help
When we die, we won't need help
But now we are homeless because of the War
PLEASE HELP US!

RAIN CLOUD

The clouds formed
Around the sun
Like a bundle of cotton wool.
The rays from the sun
Pierced the woollen balls
Like a quiet game
Of mischievous fun.
Thick black cloud
From the distance came
Shielding the piercing sun,
Turning the cotton wool
To thick black smoke
Before the heavy rain
Came tumbling down.

THE CHILDREN   *(as before)*

They stand forlorn in the war torn ruins
Silent tears falling into the burning dust
Their limbs so thin from the lack of food
Desperate now for some help and some trust.
The planes flew down from their sky of blue
The bombs had shattered the shacks they knew
as home - one room - one shelter - one life.
Now alone and forsaken - no food - no roof -
Just dust and rubble and bodies and clothes.
Everywhere broken and barren and burnt
Big sad eyes crying the only water to be found.
They are waiting for help, for love and care,
The same thing had happened within the last year.
When help does arrive it will not stay for long-
They will continue to perish, bereaved and alone
as before.

<u>IN MEMORY</u>

As the windows close on a loved one
We must always bring to mind
The beautiful memories and loving words
Of their life before they died.

Remember them always with pride
Remember them with happiness too
Their life will never be forgotten
They will always be there with you.

THE LILY

The lily is a sacred flower
I only grow it just for you
Everytime I look upon the bloom
I remember the YOU we knew.
But I don't have to look at the lily
To bring those memories of you to mind
Because as each new dawn awakens
You are always on my mind.

THE EARTHQUAKE

Into the rubble
The brave men crawled
Listening so carefully
In case someone called.

A sound or a voice
A rock's, sudden move.
Oh how they wished
They could find some life.

The Earthquake had ripped
With a terrific force,
Shredding the homes
Leaving families distraught.

How many times
Would these rescuers be,
Crawling and seeking
For 'a life', to free?

OUR DAY

Let nothing upset or distress us
In this mad busy world today
Each time we wake to greet the morn
We should all reflect and pray,
That we *CAN* get up in the morning,
That we *CAN* in fact just walk,
That we *CAN* do things for ourselves,
That we *CAN* see, and hear, and talk.

Without all these simple things in life
We would find it so very hard
Therefore, we should always remember
There are thousands of us who can't,
Walk, talk or hear or see at all,
We must be thankful in every way,
We must not let ourselves get downhearted,
But get up and get on with *OUR DAY.*

YOU FOR ME

Your words are so precious
Your love is so true,
You have made me dedicate
My complete life, to you.
I will always love and need you
So closely by my side
To be my mentor and my friend
But, to also be my guide.

NEW IMAGE

I need to get my eye lashes dyed
Along with my eyebrows and my hair.
I need my toenails and fingernails painted
And my boobs lifted to even the 'pair'!

Both my knees will need replacing
After they've done my other hip,
And I must remember to get the hair
Removed, from my upper lip.

I need a complete liposuction
And a facial peel quite quick.
My shoulders are now a bit dodgy
So they can do them after the hip.

My buttocks, they are sagging
As everything else, is going south.
I must also get the botox done,
To remove the lines, around my mouth.

All my teeth will need veneering
And wrinkles, taken from my brow.
Then maybe after all that work,
A quick, nose job, 'on the house'.

My cataracts will need removing
So I can see where I'm going, to.
'The feet' will need slightly straightening,
So I can get them in my shoes.

That just about takes care
Of my problematic body!
I want to get it all fixed up
As I don't like looking shoddy!

I hope it won't be very long
Before I get my whole new body
So I can look extremely 'glam',
For my one hundredth birthday party!

THE PRESENT

Don't look back at the past,
Just look forward to the future.
Enjoy the present and remember,
The past cannot change,
The future is unknown,
So the present is all we have.

PEACE IN THE WORLD

Peace in the World
Every day we pray
As wars erupt
Causing grief and pain
Each decade passes

Into more death and destruction
Nobody can calm these tormented shores

There will not be a peaceful World
However hard we all try
Each time we pass to better times

Wondering how long they will endure
Or whether we knew why troubles commenced
Remembering the good times and the bad
Let the whole World all pray for peaceful
Days - **FOREVER**

THE CLOUDS

The cumulus cloud
Formed a white mountain
In the distance over the sea
The shape of a dragon -
A dog - and maybe a tree.
But as the darkness fell
The white turned to grey,
And black, and pink too.
The night took my shapes,
Formed a thick black mass,
Until the moon started peeping through.
My shapes returned in a lighter form and
Back to the daytime shapes they knew.

THE LAST GOODBYE

Before I say goodbye
I want to see you.
Before I say goodbye
I want to hold you.
Before I say goodbye
I want to tell you my fear.
Before I say goodbye
I want to know you'll be there,
In that beautiful place, called Heaven, above
Where the peace and tranquillity
Spells happiness and love -
Where the trials of the World
Are finally laid to rest.
Before I say goodbye,
I want you to know,
I will always be there for **YOU**.

<u>NO LONGER</u>

No longer will I miss you
No longer will I cry
No longer will I yearn to see
The twinkle in your eye.

No longer will I hear you
No longer will I speak
No longer will I always wait
For you to come to me.

No longer will you see me
No longer will I see you
No longer will we share a thought
As we always used to do.

No longer – yes – no longer
No longer – anymore
I opened up my heart – but
Someone else has closed the door.

THE SNOWSTORM

The snowflakes fell
Glistening soft and white
Hurtling like stones
Throughout the dark night.
Blades of dark green
Pierced the carpet of white.
As dawn approached,
Awaiting the day,
The carpet of snow
Melted gently away.

THE NORFOLK BROADS

Dragonflies, Kingfishers and Cormorants
A rare but beautiful sight
The Broads in the County of Norfolk
Is where they're seen, by day or night.

Gliding swiftly over the water
Hiding away from, the holiday crowd
There on the Norfolk Broads
The locals have a need to be proud.

The waterways meander and curl
Around corners and under bridges,
The magic of the waters swirl by
Abbey Ruins and white, windmill images.

Many tales of old to tell
The sails of old Wherries revealed.
The Yachts and their Helmsmen
Turn around to show their keel.

The Marshmen still collecting
Their reeds by boat each day
The Norfolk Broads is still the home
Of hundreds of tales, you might say.

THE DAWN

The Morning came,
Before the night had gone.
The night, as usual,
Had stayed too long.
It didn't want to go.
I knew the dawn was imminent
It really seemed so slow.
Now the dawn has arrived
I don't know what to do.
I'm still alone and dreaming
And still longing to be with you.

TEMPORARY HOME

Pale but dirty concrete
Formed a floor
The walls were one,
Of a wooden door,
The others were cardboard
And concrete – that's all
The three sided shelter
Was all there was
Making a home
For the homeless
For one night - or more.

<u>ETERNAL</u>

Every day

Thoughts of you.

Every night

Recurring dreams,

Never leaving me,

Always there,

Love **ETERNAL**.

A MOMENT OF TIME

An old man shuffled along the path
Keeping just in the light of the sun
His thoughts were still bitter and dark
As his mind wandered back, one more time.

His love had left him when he was young
His children had grown up and long gone
His heart once full of passion and life
Was now – Oh so cold and so sad.

Then, perhaps by some chance, or by fate
He noticed an old lady approaching – so slow-
As she came nearer they both stopped and turned
Was it possible?   Oh yes!   It was *her* !

Even after all these years, they both knew.
Tears trickled down his old wrinkled face
The old lady – dry eyed – she just bowed,
Then she looked up, but no words were said.

They both had their own private memories
Which they both thought were now all dead
Their eyes met again, for one brief moment
But they just looked and then turned their heads.

Transfixed in that *moment of time*
The old man turned and walked on his way.
When he reached home he was very distraught
The agonies of time would not go away.

Then he gave out one last cry of pain
And after all these years, at long last
To end this long *moment of time,*
He laid down and died, from his broken heart.

HOMING IN

The robin landed on the fence
It was just then mid September
He came to find a winter home
But where? He couldn't remember
He hopped around from fence to tree
His eyes darting left and right-
He waited - listened - and then he flew
To a place he thought was quiet.
He alighted on the conifer tree
All yellow and golden leafed
The robin strutted along the branch,
"Back home" he thought "What a relief!"

THE DAY THAT NEVER CAME

I woke up this morning
Dreaming of the day
We met in the moonlight
At the end of the bay.
As we walked and talked
The evening flew away
But we never lived together
To see the next day.
How your departure tore
A big piece from me too
You left in the breeze
When really I knew
You wanted to stay,
To make a new life
But that night in the bay
Was our last night together.
I'll never forget you
The promises you made
But it wasn't your fault
As many hours I have prayed,
That this war had been kinder
And not taken your life -
As today was our wedding
To become husband and wife.

<u>IF</u>

If you ever need a friend
If you ever need an ear
If you ever need a mentor
If you ever need to share
If you ever need to cry
If you ever need to laugh
If you ever need to be
Happy, sad or lonely
Then *please* be them with me.

<u>BEAUTIFUL DAY</u>

Breaking dawn

Evening shadow

Afternoon calm

Under the clouds

Trees gently rustling

Into each other

Falling leaves

Underneath the trees

Lasting moments

Deepest thoughts

Always waiting for

You.